MANATEES

LIVING WILD

Published by Creative Education and Creative Paperbacks
P.O. Box 227, Mankato, Minnesota 56002
Creative Education and Creative Paperbacks are imprints of The Creative Company
www.thecreativecompany.us

Design and production by Mary Herrmann
Art direction by Rita Marshall
Printed in China

Photographs by Alamy (Nigel Hicks), Corbis (Luciano Candisani/Minden Pictures), Creative Commons Wikimedia (Philibert Charles Berjeau, Biodiversity Heritage Library, Creative Commons Wikimedia, Dysmachus, FunkMonk, Julius86, Joyce Kleen, Keith Ramos, SunCreator, Vassil), Dreamstime (Thediver123, Uhg1234), Getty Images (Photo Researchers), Mary Herrmann, iStockphoto (ARLipscomb, bratan007, DC_Colombia, fambros, NaluPhoto, Wilsilver77), NASA (Jacques Descloitres, Jeff Schmaltz), Shutterstock (Greg Amptman, Kipling Brock, Bulls's-Eye Arts, Filipe Frazao, fzd.it, Shane Gross, guentermanaus, Wayne Johnson, Philip Lange, Liquid Productions LLC, L. S. Luecke, Andrei Nekrassov, rook76, Sue Smith, Dennis Tokarzewski)

Library of Congress Cataloging-in-Publication Data
Gish, Melissa.
Manatees / Melissa Gish.
p. cm. — (Living wild)
Includes bibliographical references and index.
Summary: A look at manatees, including their habitats, physical characteristics such as their unique respiratory systems, behaviors, relationships with humans, and the protected status of these intelligent creatures in the world today.

ISBN 978-1-60818-705-8 (hardcover)
ISBN 978-1-62832-301-6 (pbk)
ISBN 978-1-56660-741-4 (eBook)
1. Manatees—Juvenile literature. I. Title.

QL737.S63 G57 2016
599.55—dc23   2015026824

CCSS: RI.5.1, 2, 3, 8; RST.6-8.1, 2, 5, 6, 8; RH.6-8.3, 4, 5, 6, 7, 8

First Edition HC 9 8 7 6 5 4 3 2 1
First Edition PBK 9 8 7 6 5 4 3 2 1

CREATIVE EDUCATION • CREATIVE PAPERBACKS

MANATEES

Melissa Gish

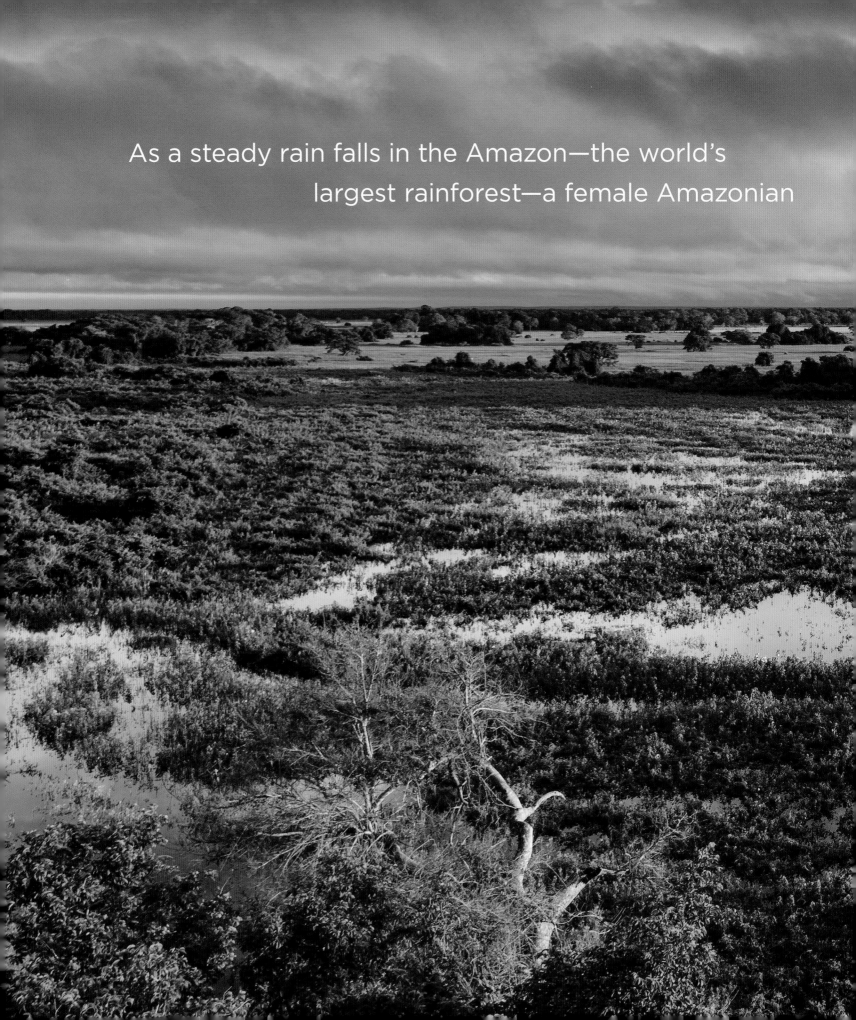

As a steady rain falls in the Amazon—the world's largest rainforest—a female Amazonian

manatee swims through the flooded wetlands.
She is preparing to give birth.

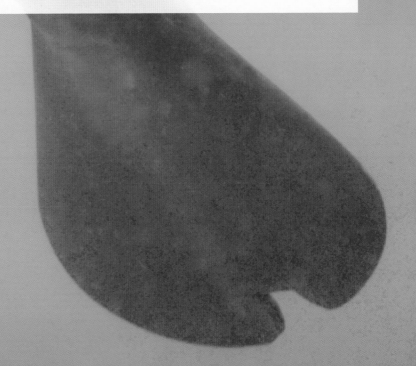

A s a steady rain falls in the Amazon—
the world's largest rainforest—a female
Amazonian manatee swims through
the flooded wetlands. She is preparing to
give birth. Safe from predators and human
interference in Brazil's Mamirauá Sustainable
Development Reserve, the manatee swims
peacefully through the shallows, using her
flippers to push off the spongy bottom. She
has timed her birthing well, as the wetlands

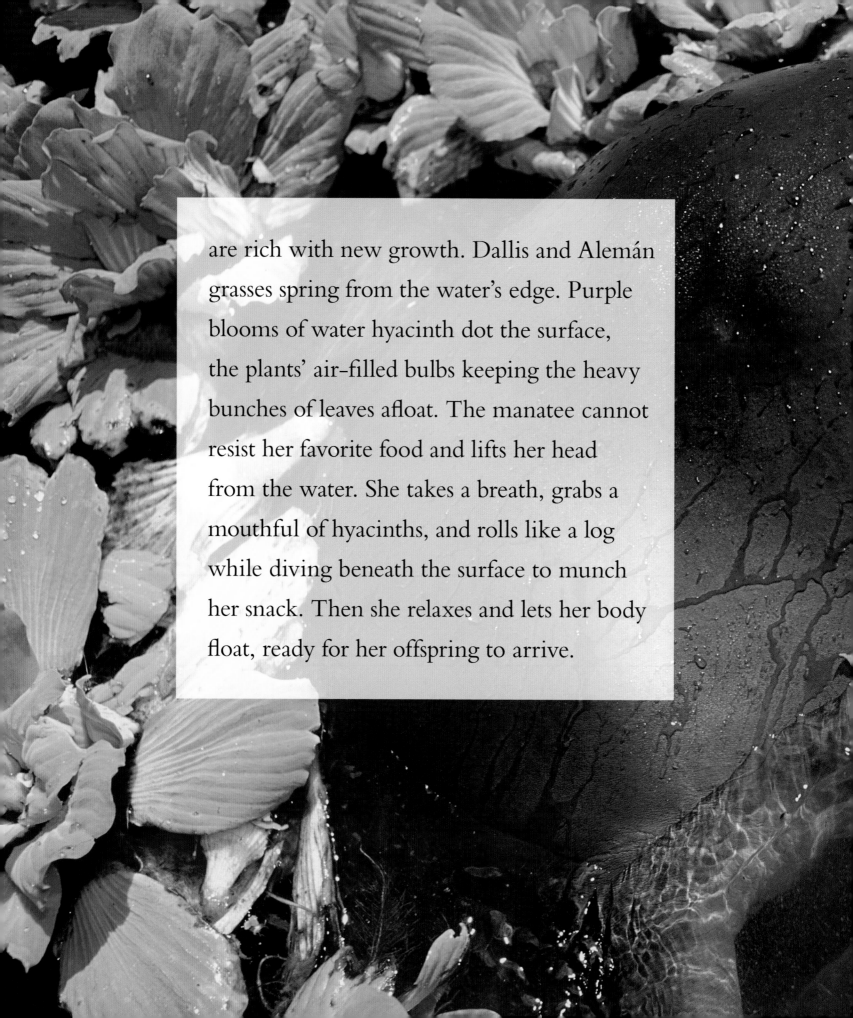

are rich with new growth. Dallis and Alemán grasses spring from the water's edge. Purple blooms of water hyacinth dot the surface, the plants' air-filled bulbs keeping the heavy bunches of leaves afloat. The manatee cannot resist her favorite food and lifts her head from the water. She takes a breath, grabs a mouthful of hyacinths, and rolls like a log while diving beneath the surface to munch her snack. Then she relaxes and lets her body float, ready for her offspring to arrive.

WHERE IN THE WORLD THEY LIVE

■ **West Indian Manatee**
coastlines and rivers
of the Caribbean,
southeastern North
America, and northern
South America

■ **African Manatee**
coastlines and rivers
of western Africa

■ **Amazonian Manatee**
Amazon Basin of
South America

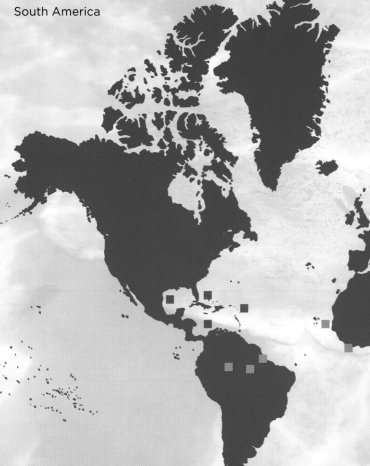

Known for their gentle disposition, the three species of manatees
inhabit the shallow waters of tropical coastlines and slow-moving
rivers. About 10,000 Amazonian manatees live in the Amazon
Basin, and roughly the same number of African manatees can
be found in western Africa. Two subspecies of the West Indian
manatee, the Antilles manatee and the Florida manatee, exist in far
fewer numbers. The colored squares represent the areas in which
each species is found.

MARVELOUS MANATEES

Moeritherium had a wide, flexible upper lip suitable for grasping vegetation, similar to modern manatees.

Because manatees are as shy as they are enormous, they are some of the least understood animals in the world. The earliest manatee ancestor, *Moeritherium*, appeared on land more than 35 million years ago and developed into more than 350 species, including the rabbit-sized hyrax, the elephant, and the manatee. Today, three manatee species exist: Amazonian, West Indian, and African. As fully aquatic animals, manatees spend their entire lives in water, inhabiting shallow **estuaries**, swamps, and slow-moving rivers. Manatees are named for their geographical distribution. Amazonian manatees are found only in freshwater habitats of the Amazon Basin. West Indian manatees fall into two subspecies: the Florida manatee, which lives in coastal areas of the southeast United States, and the Antilles manatee (also known as the Caribbean manatee), which is found in coastal areas of the Caribbean, West Indies, and Central and South America. The African manatee inhabits the coasts and rivers of West Africa from southern Mauritania to northern Angola. West Indian and African manatees can move between freshwater and saltwater habitats.

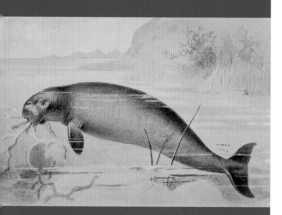

Steller's sea cow was named for German naturalist Georg Wilhelm Steller, who first described them.

Europeans hunted the Steller's sea cow, which grew to 30 feet (9.1 m) in length, and used its skin to make boats.

Manatees are members of the order Sirenia, as is their closest relative, the dugong of the Pacific and Indian oceans. A fifth Sirenian is the Steller's sea cow, which was discovered by Europeans in 1741 and hunted to **extinction** by 1768. Manatees and dugongs are sometimes called "sea cows" because of their calm nature. The word "manatee" is derived from *manatí*, which was the name given to the West Indian manatee by the **indigenous** Arawak people. The Amazonian manatee is called *peixe-boi* (*PAY-shay-BOY*) in Portuguese (the official language of Brazil), meaning "fish ox." African manatees are known as *mamiwata*, named for Mami Wata (Mother Water), a water spirit that originated in the **mythology** of coastal Nigerian people and spread to many West African **cultures**.

West Indian and African manatees can grow to 13 feet (4 m) in length and average about 1,200 pounds (544 kg), though they may weigh as much as 3,000 pounds (1,361 kg) where food is abundant. Amazonian manatees remain smaller—about 9 to 10 feet (2.7–3 m) long and rarely more than 1,000 pounds (454 kg). Females, called cows, are slightly bigger than males, called bulls. Manatees are

The dugong's snout is sharply downturned, distinguishing it from its manatee relatives.

Captive manatees are typically fed leafy greens, carrots, apples, and vitamin supplements.

herbivores, meaning they eat only plant matter. Manatees typically eat 10 to 15 percent of their body weight in aquatic vegetation every day. However, it takes them a long time to digest all that food. Because manatees often eat rough-textured plants mixed with sand, their six large cheek teeth are easily worn down. But the teeth are suited to the manatee's diet. As polyphyodonts (*PAH-lee-FY-uh-dahnts*), manatees have teeth that continuously fall out and are replaced throughout their lifetime. Having successive sets of teeth is common among fish and reptile species but rare for **mammals** except manatees and their relatives.

All mammals, with the exception of the platypus and the hedgehog-like echidna, give birth to live offspring and produce milk to feed their young. Mammals are also warm-blooded. This means that their bodies try to maintain a healthy, constant temperature that is usually warmer than their surroundings. Manatees cannot spend much time in water that is colder than 68 °F (20 °C). They breathe air through nostrils located on the top of the snout and normally hold their breath underwater for three to five minutes at a time while foraging. However,

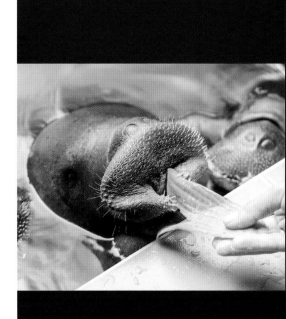

Two manatees at the Mote Marine Laboratory in Sarasota, Florida, eat 72 heads of lettuce and 12 bunches of kale per day.

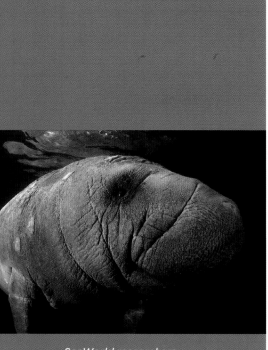

SeaWorld researchers attribute the manatee's poor sense of smell to special tissues around the nasal bones.

With each breath, humans replace about 10 percent of the air in their lungs—manatees replace about 90 percent.

when sleeping underwater, manatees can hold their breath for up to 20 minutes.

To keep from inhaling water, manatees have special muscles in their noses that pinch their nostrils tightly shut. Manatees have a breathing system that is unique among mammals. Humans' lungs are short and thick, filling the upper chest, but manatees' lungs are long and flat. They extend across 60 percent of the body length on the dorsal (back) side of the animal. In addition to aiding in breathing, the lungs function as flotation devices.

With large inner ear bones that amplify sound, manatees have good hearing. On the outside, they have tiny ear openings just behind their eyes, which are small and lack eyelids. Like most aquatic animals, manatees have a see-through inner eyelid called a nictitating (*NIK-tih-tayt-ing*) membrane that closes over each eye for protection underwater. To close their eyes, manatees contract sphincter (*SFINK-ter*) muscles around each eye, pinching the flesh closed like a fist. Although manatees have fairly good vision, their habitats are often murky. They rely heavily on the sense of touch. The manatee's entire body is covered with fine whiskers that

Manatees typically take two or three breaths in quick succession before sinking back down below the surface.

Manatee skin is silky smooth on the underbelly and rougher on the back and head.

are attached to sensitive nerves beneath the skin. These whiskers, called vibrissae, can detect vibrations caused by changes in water flow as well as objects and other animals in the water. The vibrissae on the manatee's muzzle are especially sensitive and help the animal locate food.

Like a shortened version of an elephant's trunk, the manatee's snout has a **prehensile** upper lip. Split down the center, the lip has two halves that can move independently. They work like gripping fingers, grabbing vegetation and pushing it into the mouth. On a typical day, a manatee spends 6 to 8 hours foraging for food and 8 to 10 hours sleeping. The rest of the time, it meanders through its habitat. The manatee has no hind limbs. It uses its paddle-like tail and its front flippers to swim or walk along the bottom of its shallow aquatic home. While each flipper is smooth, the bones inside form five distinct digits, resembling those of a human hand. Protruding slightly from the ends of West Indian and African manatee flippers are fingernails, which help the manatee keep its grip as it moves along sandy surfaces.

Despite their bulk, manatees have very little body fat and can suffer frostbite and hypothermia (being too cold) in cold temperatures. When winter approaches, a manatee's instinct tells it to **migrate** to warmer waters. In North America, manatees from North Carolina to Texas gather in Florida, swimming up slow-moving rivers and streams that lead to natural springs, where the water averages 72 °F to 74 °F (22.2 to 23.3 °C) all winter. When spring arrives, the manatees once again head to the coasts.

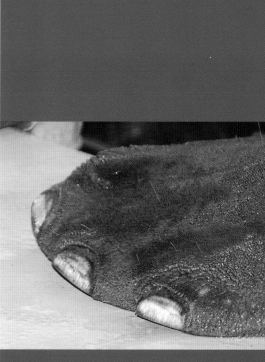

The manatee's fingernails are similar in appearance and skeletal structure to the toenails of an elephant.

Manatee rib bones are dense and lack bone marrow, so manatees easily sink when their lungs are not filled with air.

A recent study from the
Netherlands suggests manatees'
slow-moving lifestyle may help
protect them from cancer.

COWS OF THE SEA

Curved flippers help manatees move forward and roll onto their sides and back while swimming.

A lthough manatees spend most of their time alone, foraging and sleeping, they are social animals that freely share habitat with little regard for one another—much like cows grazing together in a pasture. Social groups vary in number from five to several dozen manatees. Generally shy around other animals and people, manatees communicate mostly by touch. Manatees sometimes play together, rubbing faces or flippers and nudging each other for a slow game of chase.

Manatees are usually quiet but sometimes vocalize underwater using complex patterns of chirps and squeaks. They announce their presence to one another with simple squeaks. To express annoyance, a series of short chirps seems to say, "Buzz off!" And when manatees are frightened, their squeaks become long and shrill—similar to human screaming.

Males tend to vocalize more during mating periods, warning away other males while calling to females. The closest bonds and most frequent vocal communications occur between a manatee mother and her baby, called a calf, who learns to recognize its mother's voice. Driven

Physical contact is an important part of calves' social development and species communication.

by no specific mating season, female manatees can give birth at any time of the year. However, food availability and weather patterns play roles in reproduction.

Not all females mate at the same time, though most mating occurs in spring or early summer. Females are old enough to mate by age five. When the time is right for a particular female, her body produces special **hormones** that attract males, who are ready to mate by age nine. Males compete to be the first to mate with a selected female. Five or six males will gather around one or two females, pushing each other and vocalizing to get closest to the females. A female will mate with several males to ensure the best chance of conceiving a calf.

Females mate only once every two to five years. Successful mating is vital to the species' survival. An otherwise healthy female who is stressed because of habitat disturbance, lack of food, or cold weather will not mate. After a manatee conceives, she carries her calf for 12 months before giving birth. Normally, only one calf is born, but rare cases of twins have been reported. Depending on the age and size of its mother, a newborn manatee calf ranges from 3 to 4 feet (0.9–1.2 m) in length and between 60 and 70 pounds (27.2–31.8 kg) in weight.

Immediately, the calf can swim and hold its breath underwater. For the first few weeks, its mother must help lift it to the surface to take each breath. It swims and rests beside its mother while suckling milk from the two nipples located behind her flippers. Within a few weeks, the calf begins eating plants, while its mother's nourishing milk supplements its vegetarian diet for the next 18 to 24 months. A mother and her calf are inseparable. Even when the young manatee becomes an adult, it may remain in its mother's social group, its bond with her

The algae on manatees' backs protects the animals' skin from potential sunburn.

Because algae grow in sunny conditions on wet surfaces, these organisms are often found on manatees' backs.

Research has shown that captive manatee calves may grow at slower rates than wild calves in the first year.

unbroken for life. Such a relationship is similar to that of elephants, which form family groups that include several generations of animals.

Manatees in captivity usually live up to 60 years, but some have lived longer than 65 years. However, few survive more than 25 years in the wild, and conservationists have found that many die before reaching the age of 10. While adult manatees have no natural predators, their lives are often cut short by pollution and starvation related to habitat destruction, sudden periods of cold weather resulting from global **climate change**, and conflict with humans.

Calves are especially vulnerable. Young manatees are often attacked by large predators such as alligators, crocodiles, snapping turtles, and great white and bull sharks. In addition, calves are curious and may eat trash or other **toxic** materials, which can poison them or get stuck in their digestive system. Because calves cannot hold their breath as long as adults, they and their mother must remain close to the water's surface most of the time. This makes them vulnerable to boat strikes—a major cause of manatee mortality in both adults and calves.

Manatee calves learn everything, from social behaviors to food choices, from their mothers.

In Florida, 25 percent of manatee deaths are caused by collisions with boats.

Despite all the dangers of life in the wild, humans continue to pose the greatest threat to manatees. In Africa, manatees are hunted for **bushmeat**, even though they are a protected species in several countries. And unlike their cousins in North and South America, African manatees sometimes eat fish and shellfish, which they may discover in fishing nets. Manatees often become entangled in the nets and either drown or die at the hands of angry fishermen. Also, water levels vary more in Africa than in other manatee habitats. Manatees may find themselves trapped and starving in shrinking pools or streams as the heat of summer increases.

Amazonian manatees are hunted for food and get trapped in fishing nets as well, but their greatest challenge is finding suitable homes in an environment that is being reshaped on a daily basis. Manatees are being pushed into ever-shrinking habitats as dams are built and swampland is drained to make way for urban development, agriculture, and industry in South America. The Amazonian and African manatees each have a population of about 10,000 and are classified as vulnerable by the International Union for Conservation of Nature (IUCN).

About 2,000 Antilles manatees exist, and roughly 5,000 Florida manatees remain. The Florida manatee was added to the U.S. Fish & Wildlife Service Endangered Species List in 1967. However, U.S. officials are now considering its removal from the list despite a steady decline in its numbers. In 2013 alone, 16 percent of the state's manatees died, and scientists cannot explain why. Further, in 2014, the IUCN issued a warning that the Florida manatee population could fall by another 20 percent over the next 40 years. Both the Florida and Antilles manatees are classified as endangered by the IUCN.

Large groups of manatees that gather seasonally in hot springs to avoid cold weather are called aggregations.

Edvard Eriksen's statue of the Little Mermaid in Copenhagen, Denmark, was based on the famous Danish fairy tale.

MERMAID MYSTERY

T he order of manatees and dugongs is named for the sirens of Greek mythology, beautiful women later portrayed in Roman mythology as mermaids. Manatees, dugongs, and mermaids have a long history together. The first mermaid appeared in a 3,000-year-old story from Assyria (an ancient empire that spanned an area from present-day Egypt to Azerbaijan). Atargatis was a beautiful goddess who fell in love with a shepherd. Her powers were so strong that she accidentally killed her lover and, overcome with grief, threw herself into a river. As punishment, she wanted to turn into a fish. However, her beauty was too great to transform fully, and only a fish's tail grew to replace her lower body. From that story, myths and legends of mermaids emerged in nearly every culture of the world.

Hawaiian fishers told stories about Hina puku i'a, a mermaid whom they believed protected them at sea. Japanese fishers thought that mermaids called Ningen could cry tears that transformed into pearls. While some stories portrayed mermaids as vain and deceitful, most artists and poets continued associating mermaids with

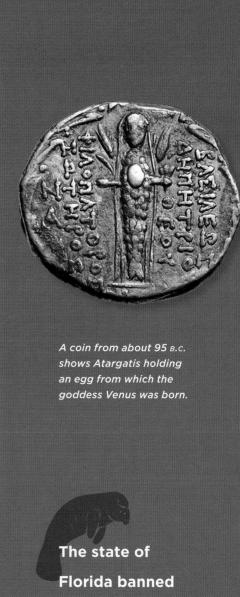

A coin from about 95 B.C. shows Atargatis holding an egg from which the goddess Venus was born.

The state of Florida banned the hunting of manatees in 1893, after the species was nearly wiped out.

Residents of Key West, Florida, are known for displaying unique manatee mailboxes.

Manatees are drawn to waters near power plants because the seawater they pump out stays warm all winter.

beauty. Such images were alive in the minds of explorers and their crews as they traveled to the New World (the Americas) in the 15th and 16th centuries.

In 1493, as Columbus sailed near what is now the Dominican Republic, he encountered several creatures that he reported as mermaids. Columbus wrote that "some female forms rose high out of the sea but were not as beautiful as they are represented, for somehow the face looked more like a man's." In reality, the creatures Columbus saw were manatees. Reported sightings of manatees and dugongs mistaken for mermaids became commonplace as more Europeans traveled across the oceans of the Southern Hemisphere. English explorer John Smith wrote that the "mermaids" he spotted in 1614 were "by no means unattractive" and caused him to "experience the first effects of love."

Soon, however, manatees and dugongs were taken out of love poems and put on the dinner menu. A 1739 article in *The Scots Magazine* described how the English crew of the ship *Halifax*, sailing a trade route in the East Indies, had caught and eaten several mermaids. Back in London, the crew reported that the creatures had moaned "with

great sensibility when caught" and tasted similar to veal, or young cattle. Historians believe the *Halifax*'s mermaids were dugongs, which do taste like veal.

While Amazonian and African manatees are still killed for food today, West Indian manatees encounter more tourists than hunters. In 1975, the state of Florida designated the manatee as the official state marine mammal, and efforts to educate people about these gentle giants began in earnest. The public was invited to visit—and swim in—the warm waters of such manatee wintering grounds as Crystal River Preserve State Park and Homosassa Springs Wildlife State Park on Florida's

The Sanctuary for the Marine Mammals of Citrus County takes people swimming with manatees.

THE MERMAID

1

Who would be
A mermaid fair,
Singing alone,
Combing her hair
Under the sea,
In a golden curl
With a comb of pearl,
On a throne?

2

I would be a mermaid fair;
I would sing to myself the whole of the day;
With a comb of pearl I would comb my hair;
And still as I comb'd I would sing and say,
"Who is it loves me? who loves not me?"
I would comb my hair till my ringlets would fall,

Low adown, low adown,
From under my starry sea-bud crown
Low adown and around,
And I should look like a fountain of gold
Springing alone
With a shrill inner sound,
Over the throne
In the midst of the hall;
Till that great sea-snake under the sea
From his coiled sleeps in the central deeps
Would slowly trail himself sevenfold
Round the hall where I sate, and look in at the gate
With his large calm eyes for the love of me.
And all the mermen under the sea
Would feel their immortality
Die in their hearts for the love of me . . .

from "The Mermaid" *by Alfred Tennyson (1809–92)*

east coast and Blue Springs State Park in central Florida. The manatee is protected by the Florida Manatee Sanctuary Act of 1978, which makes it "unlawful for any person, at any time, intentionally or negligently, to annoy, molest, harass, or disturb any manatee."

The U.S. Fish and Wildlife Service enforces no-feeding and no-touching rules where people and manatees come together. Swimmers are encouraged to float on the water's surface and allow manatees to move naturally around them. Manatees are not aggressive, and there are no records of manatees biting people. However, if a manatee feels threatened by someone behaving badly toward it, the manatee will attempt to flee. In doing so, it could harm the person with its enormous body or powerful tail. Feeding manatees can disrupt their natural behavior, causing them to lose their fear of people and boats. It could even make them seek out people in hopes of food, which could increase the risk of boat collisions. Touching manatees or their calves could frighten them away from warm-water areas and put them in danger of frostbite or hypothermia in winter waters that are too cold. Anyone caught feeding or touching manatees could face a fine or even jail time.

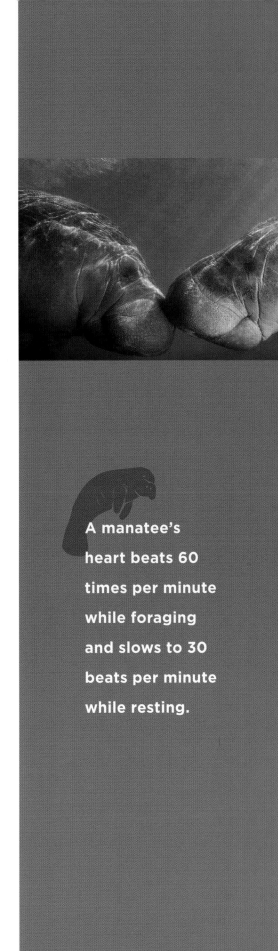

A manatee's heart beats 60 times per minute while foraging and slows to 30 beats per minute while resting.

The Amazonian manatee was featured on postage stamps from Brazil in 1979.

The state of Florida has created manatee observation areas at parks all around the state so that people can safely enjoy watching manatees in their natural habitat.

Another way to see manatees is online. Save the Manatee Club (SMC) is an organization established in 1981 by singer/songwriter Jimmy Buffett and former U.S. senator Bob Graham when he was governor of Florida. SMC not only provides information about West Indian manatees but also hosts a live webcam on its website, www.savethemanatee.org. From November to April, the live stream features the manatees as they swim at Blue Springs State Park. Other times of the year, the site streams previously recorded footage.

Modern stories about manatees are an important method of educating the public on these aquatic animals. John Hughes's 2014 book *Gumbo the Talking Manatee* tells the story of a boy who finds a stranded Florida manatee calf and helps save its life. Gumbo is housed with other rescued manatees at SeaWorld, where he grows strong enough to be released into the wild at Three Sisters Springs, Florida. A real-life manatee, Snooty, the first Florida manatee born in captivity, is featured in the 2008

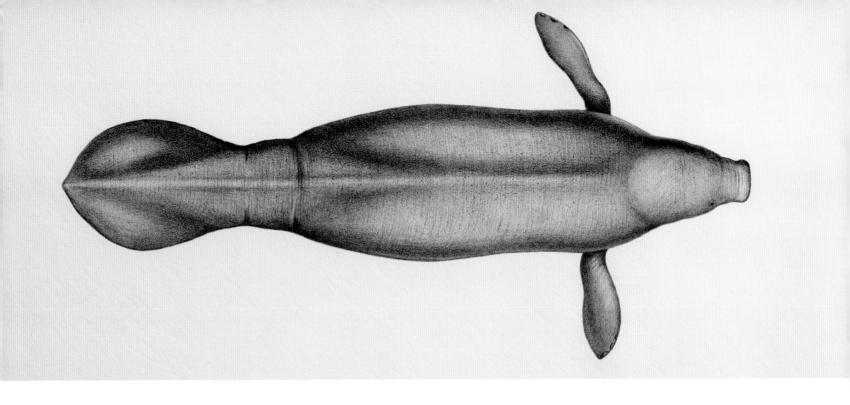

book *Florida's Famous Animals* by Jan Annino. Born in Miami on July 21, 1948, Snooty later moved to South Florida Museum's Parker Manatee Aquarium. As of 2016, Snooty was the oldest captive manatee on record. Annino's book tells Snooty's life story and includes photographs of Snooty and his adopted manatee family.

Commemorative postage stamps are another tool that can be used to assist in wildlife awareness and conservation. From the U.S. to Ghana to the Republic of Togo, countries around the world have featured endangered manatees on their stamps. In 1992, the island of Anguilla released a stamp commemorating the 500th anniversary of Columbus's voyage to the New World. It featured a reproduction of a historic map and Columbus's drawing of a "mermaid"—the manatee.

Manatees were featured in an 1885 publication from the Zoological Society of London, a conservation organization.

Research conducted in manatees' native habitats is vital to developing protection and conservation strategies.

MANATEES NEED US

Manatees simply cannot reproduce fast enough to replace their numbers when so many losses occur year after year. Manatees face enormous pressure from nature. Global climate change has been affecting ocean temperatures, weather patterns, and storm intensity—all of which in turn influence manatee behavior and health. Manatees thrive in warm water, but water that is too warm for too long can lead to the overgrowth of algae, which can be deadly to manatees. Several species of algae are toxic. Massive overgrowth, or blooms, of certain species of brown and red algae are called red tides. The algae stick to the sea grasses that manatees eat. The toxins in the algae damage the manatees' nervous system, **paralyzing** the animals and causing them to drown. Red tides have been increasing in recent years. In 2010, red tides in the Gulf of Mexico led to the deaths of 766 Florida manatees. Three years later, red tides killed another 803 manatees. If treated early, manatees stricken with red tide poisoning can be saved with **antibiotics** and atropine, a drug used to slow nerve responses by relaxing muscles.

A view from space shows a massive algae bloom surrounding the coastline of Florida.

A 2000 study conducted by USGS researcher Dr. Iske Larkin found that manatees take seven days to digest a meal.

Manatees swim about 5 miles (8 km) per hour but are capable of going 20 miles (32.2 km) per hour for short bursts.

An increase in dramatic weather **fluctuations**, including colder winters that arrive earlier, can leave manatees stranded in cold water. In 2010, a colder-than-normal winter led to the deaths of 246 Florida manatees. In late December 2013 and early January 2014, three Florida manatees were rescued from the St. Johns River in Jacksonville. Typically, manatees have until February to make their way to the springs in the central and southern parts of the state before winter weather strikes. However, by late December 2013, the manatees had become cold-stressed and were close to death. After more than a year at SeaWorld, where they received medical treatment and special diets to increase their weight, the manatees—whom the Animal Rescue Team named Sissy, Bycatch, and Wallace—were released at Blue Springs State Park. Many manatees are rescued and rehabilitated by SeaWorld and other organizations. Without their assistance, manatee numbers would undoubtedly be much lower than current estimates.

Another effect of global climate change is an increase in the frequency and intensity of ocean storms. As coastal-dwelling animals, manatees are especially vulnerable to tropical storms and hurricanes. The U.S.

Geological Survey (USGS) is the government agency responsible for studying Earth's natural resources and hazards, including hurricanes. In 2007, a team of USGS wildlife biologists and geologists published the results of a study on West Indian manatees and hurricanes. The study found that manatees seem to know when extreme weather is on its way. They avoid travel and instead remain in one place to ride out storms.

The manatees' "hunker down" strategy works for most tropical storms, but when the storms become hurricanes, survival becomes more challenging. Manatees in coastal

Benefiting from the sun's warming rays, manatees sometimes swim belly-up near the water's surface.

As water drains off roads and developed land, it carries with it oil, chemicals, and other harmful materials.

areas may be swept out to sea by violent waves. Or they may become stranded on shore when floodwaters recede. Manatees can also be injured or killed by debris in the water, as hurricanes often destroy houses and other structures. In addition, chemicals or other toxins spilled during a hurricane may **contaminate** manatee habitats.

Perhaps the foremost authority on Florida manatees is Dr. Robert Bonde, who has been studying manatees since 1978. Because nearly every Florida manatee has encountered at least one motorboat in its lifetime and bears the visible scars of that encounter, Bonde photographs manatees' scars in order to identify individuals. Combining his photos with **genetic** data drawn from the animals' blood and tissue samples, Bonde has contributed to studies concerned with the health and diversity of Florida's manatee population.

To learn how manatees behave in their habitat, Bonde relies on **Global Positioning System** (GPS) devices that are temporarily clipped to a manatee's tail. Each device sends an electronic signal that can be picked up by a weather **satellite**, allowing Bonde to map an individual manatee's movements. The GPS device is attached to a buoy (a floating object) by a thin rope. This way, researchers can easily locate the device and remove it from the manatee when it is no longer needed. Since 2009, Dr. Bonde's research has expanded to include manatees in Belize and Puerto Rico, and other manatee researchers in Brazil, Mexico, and West Africa have adopted his methods.

The African manatee is the most endangered and least understood of the three manatee species. In 2006, after studying West Indian manatees in the U.S. for 10 years,

The U.S. Fish and Wildlife Service estimates that only about 60 percent of boaters observe manatee safety signs.

African manatees inhabit the rivers and coastlines of 21 countries and are found as far as 2,000 miles (3,219 km) inland in rivers of Mali and Chad.

biologist Dr. Lucy Keith Diagne moved to Gabon to study African manatees. Working with scientists from several African countries, Diagne's research in Gabon and Senegal covers a broad range of questions on the manatee, including behavior, feeding habits, and habitat use. For the first time, GPS technology was used to track and study African manatees to help determine their numbers and distribution. Diagne's project also includes the first large-scale genetics and aging study of the African manatee. In addition to studying manatees in the wild, Diagne provides training and educational outreach. Save the Manatee Club helped Diagne develop a manatee coloring book and stickers for use at schools and other public presentations. The materials are in French—the common language of Gabon. Diagne also is working with two natural history museums to create permanent educational displays about manatees.

One question researchers have only begun to address is that of manatee intelligence. Scientists have long believed that brain size plays a role in human and animal intelligence. Because manatees have the smallest brain-to-body-size ratio of any mammal, it was assumed they were not very smart. However, Dr. Roger L. Reep, a

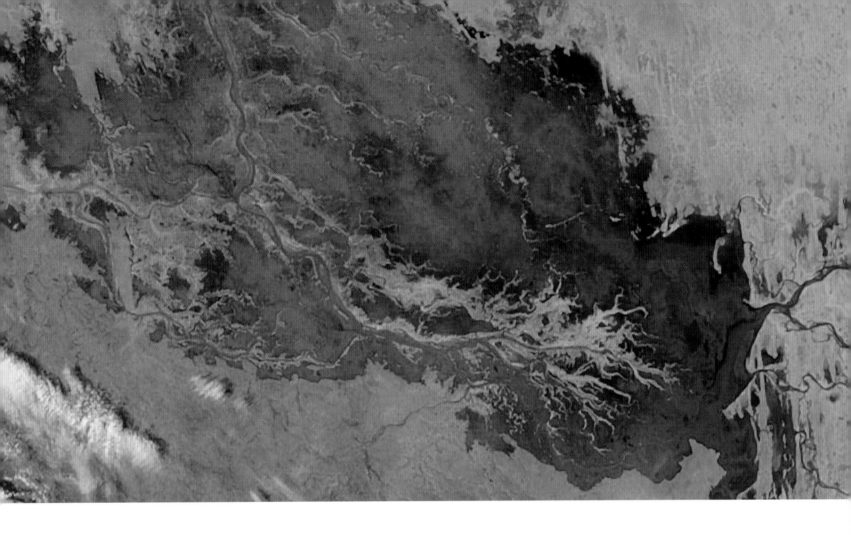

The tributaries and mangrove swamps of the Niger Delta (shown from space) are home to most of Africa's manatees.

neuroscientist at the University of Florida at Gainesville, has learned otherwise. He believes that since manatees have no need to hunt and are not forced to outsmart predators, the manatee's brain simply stayed small over the millennia as the body continued to **evolve** into a larger size. Reep found that, despite being slow moving, manatees are as quick to learn as dolphins—perhaps one more reason to appreciate these shy aquatic creatures. Humans must remain dedicated to research and conservation in order to protect manatees around the world from the many dangers they face on our changing planet.

ANIMAL TALE: HOW THE MANATEE CAME TO BE

Legends of sailors and explorers mistaking manatees for mermaids have persisted throughout history. Some stories tell of these mythic creatures, known as *rusalkas* in Russia, luring sailors to their doom on rocky shores. Others depict mermaids, called *navmands* in Scandinavia, as magical beings that traded pearls to treasure hunters. A Portuguese legend suggests how the connection between manatees and mermaids may have begun.

Long ago, a young man named Diego wished to leave Portugal and see what lay beyond the horizon. He joined a crew of explorers and set sail for Africa. For many weeks, their ship traveled over the waves, pushed southward by a steady wind.

When the ship reached the tropical waters off the coast of Sierra Leone, a ferocious storm tossed the ship

mercilessly. As the sea raged, Diego and the other men struggled to keep the ship safe. Suddenly, a massive wave washed over the deck and swept Diego into the sea. The sky was filled with clouds, blotting out the moonlight, and the wind howled like a ghostly animal. No one could see or hear Diego. He was lost.

Diego struggled against the crushing waves, flailing his arms and kicking his legs, but he soon became exhausted. He slipped into the blackness of the sea. As he drifted downward, the water became still and calm. Diego could see shadows spinning around him. He felt hands pulling at his arms.

When Diego awoke, he was on the beach. The storm had passed, and the full moon shone brightly in the night sky. In the distance, Diego could see his ship anchored in

the bay. He saw a young woman swimming near the shore, and he waded out into the water to ask her what had happened. She admitted to being the one who had saved him during the storm.

Diego rejoined his shipmates when they arrived on land. As the men explored the tropical paradise, Diego found himself drawn to the shore every night to see the beautiful woman who had saved him from drowning. She never left the water, though, and finally Diego asked her the reason. She explained that she was half fish—a mermaid—and she could never leave the water. Diego did not mind that she was different. He told her that he loved her.

The explorers discovered many wonderful treasures—birds, monkeys, fruits, and gemstones—which they loaded onto their ship for the return voyage to Portugal. When the

time came to leave, Diego begged the woman to return to Portugal with him. She said she could not leave the warm waters of her homeland. Cold water would kill her. Diego was heartbroken.

Then the woman suggested she make a heavy coat to wear in the cold waters of Portugal. It could be done, but it would take some time. This made Diego very happy, and although he had to leave, he promised to return for her. The woman set to work making her heavy coat.

Alas, Diego's ship met a sad fate on its return voyage. A storm dashed it against the rocks, and all the men were killed. To this day, the mermaid wearing a heavy coat—the manatee—swims slowly up and down the coast of Sierra Leone, waiting for Diego to return.

GLOSSARY

antibiotics – medicines that kill or disable the growth of bacteria, or living organisms that cannot be seen except under a microscope

bushmeat – the meat of wild animals killed for food or for sale in tropical parts of the world such as Asia and Africa

climate change – the gradual increase in Earth's temperature that causes changes in the planet's atmosphere, environments, and long-term weather conditions

contaminate – to negatively affect by exposure to a polluting substance

cultures – particular groups in a society that share behaviors and characteristics that are accepted as normal by that group

estuaries – the mouths of large rivers, where the tides (from oceans or seas) meet the streams

evolve – to gradually develop into a new form

extinction – the act or process of becoming extinct; coming to an end or dying out

fluctuations – irregular risings and fallings in number or amount

genetic – relating to genes, the basic physical units of heredity

Global Positioning System – a system of satellites, computers, and other electronic devices that work together to determine the location of objects or living things that carry a trackable device

hormones – chemical substances produced in the body that control and regulate the activity of certain cells and organs

indigenous – originating in a particular region or country

mammals – warm-blooded animals that have a backbone and hair or fur, give birth to live young, and produce milk to feed their young

migrate – to undertake a regular, seasonal journey from one place to another and then back again

mythology – a collection of myths, or popular, traditional beliefs or stories that explain how something came to be or that are associated with a person or object

neuroscientist – one who studies how the body's nervous system and brain work

paralyzing – resulting in a loss of muscle movement

prehensile – capable of grasping

satellite – a mechanical device launched into space; it may be designed to travel around Earth or toward other planets or the sun

toxic – harmful or poisonous

SELECTED BIBLIOGRAPHY

Defenders of Wildlife. "Fact Sheet: Florida Manatee." http://www.defenders.org/florida-manatee/basic-facts.

Marsh, Helene, Thomas J. O'Shea, and John E. Reynolds III. *Ecology and Conservation of the Sirenia: Dugongs and Manatees*. New York: Cambridge University Press, 2012.

National Geographic. "Manatee." http://animals.nationalgeographic.com/animals/mammals/manatee.

Reep, Roger L., and Robert K. Bonde. *The Florida Manatee: Biology and Conservation*. Gainesville: University Press of Florida, 2010.

Ripple, Jeff. *Manatees and Dugongs of the World*. Stillwater, Minn.: Voyageur Press, 1999.

Save the Manatee Club. "Resources for Students." http://www.savethemanatee.org/ed_student_resources.html.

Note: Every effort has been made to ensure that any websites listed above were active at the time of publication. However, because of the nature of the Internet, it is impossible to guarantee that these sites will remain active indefinitely or that their contents will not be altered.

Knowing more about manatees' needs helps people make decisions as they develop areas near the coast.

INDEX

activities 7–8, 15–16, 19, 21, 23–24, 26, 27, 38, 42
    breathing 8, 15–16, 19, 23, 24
    eating 8, 15, 19, 21, 23, 24, 26
    migrating 19, 27, 38
    sleeping 16, 19, 21
    swimming 7–8, 19, 23, 38

African manatees 10, 11, 12, 19, 26, 27, 31, 41–42

Amazonian manatees 7–8, 10, 11, 12, 27, 31, 41

aquariums 35
    Parker Manatee Aquarium 35

calves 15, 21, 23–24

communication 21–23

conservation and research efforts 15, 24, 27, 31, 33–34, 37–43
    by Dr. Robert Bonde 40–41
    by Dr. Lucy Keith Diagne 42
    and GPS technology 41, 42
    International Union for Conservation of Nature 27
    Mote Marine Laboratory 15
    by Dr. Roger L. Reep 42–43
    Save the Manatee Club 34, 42
    SeaWorld 38
    state of Florida 31, 33–34
    U.S. Fish & Wildlife Service 27, 33
    U.S. Geological Survey 37, 38–39

cultural influences 12, 29–30, 32, 34–35, 44–45
    on explorers 29–30
    literature 29–30, 32, 34–35
    mythologies 12, 29, 44–45
    postage stamps 35

dangers 12, 23, 24, 26–27, 29–31, 33, 37–41, 43
    habitat disruption 23, 24, 26–27, 37–38, 40
    harmful substances 24, 26, 37, 40
    humans 12, 24, 26–27, 29–31, 33, 41
        boating 24, 26, 33, 41
        hunting 12, 26–27, 29–31
    pollution 24, 37, 40
    predators 24
    starvation 23, 24, 26
    weather 23, 24, 37–40

diets 8, 15, 19, 23–24, 26, 37–38, 42
    and digestion 15, 24, 37
    fish and shellfish 26
    plants 8, 15, 19, 23

habitats 7, 10, 11, 15–16, 19, 21, 26–27, 29, 31, 33–34, 38–42
    Caribbean 10, 11
    coastlines 10, 11, 19, 38–39, 42
    estuaries 11
    North America 10, 11, 19, 27, 29, 31, 33, 41
        Florida 19, 27, 29, 31, 33, 41
    rivers and streams 10, 11, 19, 26, 38, 42
    South America 7, 10, 11, 27
        Amazon Basin 7, 10, 11
    West Africa 10, 11, 26, 42
    wetlands 7, 11

intelligence 42–43

life expectancy 24, 35, 37

mating 21–23

physical characteristics 7, 11, 12, 15–16, 18–19, 21, 23, 33, 41–43
    flippers 7, 19, 21, 23
    lungs 16, 19
    senses 16, 18
    sizes 11, 12, 16, 19, 23, 33, 43
    snouts 15–16, 18–19
    tails 19, 33, 41
    teeth 15
    toenails 19
    vibrissae 16, 18

populations 27, 29, 37–38, 41–42

protected areas 7, 31, 33–34, 38
    Florida state parks 31, 33–34, 38
    Mamirauá Sustainable Development Reserve 7

relatives 11, 12, 15, 29–31
    dugongs 12, 29, 30–31
    Moeritherium 11
    Steller's sea cows 12

Sirenia order 12, 29

social behaviors 21–24, 27, 33, 41–42

speeds 38, 43

water temperatures 15, 19, 23, 27, 30, 33, 37, 38

West Indian manatees 10, 11, 12, 19, 27, 31, 34, 37–41
    Antilles manatees 11, 27
    Florida manatees 11, 27, 34, 37–38, 40–41